Limerositus

Stephen Evans

"I wish it need not have happened in my time"

—Frodo Baggins

This is a work of verse. The names, characters, places, and incidents are either the products of the author's imagination or are used fictitiously, and any resemblance to actual persons living or dead, business establishments, events, or locales is entirely coincidental.

Book Layout ©2017 BookDesignTemplates.com

ISBN: 978-1-953725-26-4

Limerositus/ Stephen Evans —1st edition

Time Being Media LLC.

Contents

Foreword

Philosophy translates from the Greek into love of wisdom. I don't know how much wisdom there is in it, but I have always been attracted to it, not the ideal life so much as a life of ideas.

This little book likely has no wisdom in it, but perhaps the fact of it will demonstrate an appreciation for those men who spent their lives in this way. Though the fact that fewer women have done the same (or at least have not become famous for doing it) probably tells you it's not a very wise thing to do.

But the idea of unwisely spending your life searching for wisdom makes me smile. I think a limerick is the perfect form for expressing that feeling.

I hope they make you smile as well.

STEPHEN EVANS

Arendt

"In an ever-changing, incomprehensible world the masses had reached the point where they would, at the same time, believe everything and nothing."

Hannah Arendt,
The Origins of Totalitarianism

Hanna was humming a Tune

Which ballooned to a kind of a Croon

In beginnings Abound

Every wonderful Sound

As she belted out clear to the Moon

STEPHEN EVANS

Aristotle

"Freedom is obedience to self-formulated rules."

—Aristotle
The Nicomachean Ethics

Aristotle had just the right Name

Which I think was a part of his Fame

For as Melvin his Thought

Though impeccably Taught

Just wouldn't have sounded the Same

STEPHEN EVANS

Aurelius

"The first rule is to keep an untroubled spirit. The second is to look things in the face and know them for what they are."

—Marcus Aurelius
Meditations

Old Marcus as emperor Sure

Was wise in the ways of Grandeur

But his words were not Grand

Nor written in Sand

And his wisdom will simply Endure

S<small>TEPHEN</small> E<small>VANS</small>

Bentham

"Prejudice apart, the game of push-pin is of equal value with the arts and sciences of music and poetry."

Jeremy Bentham
The Rationale of Reward

Bentham was gazing Around

At prisons he thought were Unsound

Yet at Battersea Rise

With a Word from the Wise

The ground in his vision Unwound

STEPHEN EVANS

Bergson

"A philosopher worthy of the name never says more than one thing"

Henri Bergson
Creative Evolution

Henri was a man of his Time
Who evolved into something Sublime
He laughed with Elan
At the vital Raison
As the D'etre of creation's Climb

Berkeley

"To be is to be perceived."

—George Berkeley
The Principles of Human Knowledge

When Berkeley was being Ordained
As bishop, he soundly Explained
That a tree when it Falls
Sounds like nothing at All
Which is probably why he Abstained

STEPHEN EVANS

Camus

"An intellectual is someone whose mind watches itself"

Albert Camus
Carnets

Camus était penser de Vous

Who have never encountered a Clue

There is happiness Still

In the rock and the Hill

Surtout pour les hommes plus têtu

STEPHEN EVANS

Chomsky

"The smart way to keep people passive and obedient is to strictly limit the spectrum of acceptable opinion, but allow very lively debate within that spectrum...."

—Noam Chomsky,
The Common Good

Noam is never Bereft

In detecting the warp in the Weft

His mind is so Pure

His opinions Obscure

May untangle the right in the Left

Stephen Evans

Confucius

"The man who moves a mountain begins by carrying away small stones."

—Confucius,
The Analects

The Master was never Alone

For Kong as he liked to be Known

Would never not Do

Nothing not nicely To

No one nearly not known as his Own

S<small>TEPHEN</small> E<small>VANS</small>

de Beauvoir

"One is not born, but rather becomes, a woman."

> —*Simone de Beauvoir*
> *The Second Sex*

Simone sounded something Profound

But found there was no one Around

A woman she Taught

Must create her own Ought

And ought to be taught out of Bound

STEPHEN EVANS

Derrida

"And still the text will remain, if it is really cryptic and parodying (and I tell you that it is so through and through...)"

—Jacques Derrida
Spurs: Nietzsche's Styles

Derrida derailed his Duress

Deconstructing phenomenal Mess

Ages as a Sign

He would often Opine

That a work was a Meta-Process

STEPHEN EVANS

Dewey

*"Every great advance in science has issued
from a new audacity of imagination."*

—John Dewey
The Quest for Certainty

Dewey is certainly Not

The Decimal guy as you Thought

His system was Found

To be functionally Sound

Which normally matters a Lot

STEPHEN EVANS

Emerson

"Do your work."

Ralph Waldo Emerson
Self-Reliance

Old Waldo was sailing Away
But his mind could not carry the Day
Still his words would Remain
For the humans Humane
To illumine the rest of the Way

STEPHEN EVANS

Epictetus

"Aiming therefore at such great things, remember that you must not allow yourself to be carried, even with a slight tendency, towards the attainment of lesser things."

Epictetus
The Enchiridion

A tasty retreat the man Made

When from Lemons he made Lemonade

Though his leg became Lame

His unbearable Fame

Led him haltingly Anterograde

STEPHEN EVANS

Epimenides

"Cretans are always liars"

Epimenides
Cretica

Epimendides' fingers were Crossed
When he said as he found himself Lost
That a Liar was He
Who from Knossos by Sea
Did embark on a lark Tempest-Tossed.

STEPHEN EVANS

Evans

"Or you can think of me as a theoretical comedian."

—Stephen Evans
Funny Thing Is

There once was a thinker named Evans

Who meant his ideas for the Heavens

But his thoughts had no Wings

So he tied them with Strings

To Balloons found at Sixes and Sevens

STEPHEN EVANS

Foucault

"The judges of normality are present everywhere."

—Michel Foucault
Discipline and Punish

Foucault was a writer per Force
Whom the powers declined to Endorse
For his thought was so Dense
It was almost past Tense
As the words emerged without Remorse

STEPHEN EVANS

Gödel

"To every ω-consistent recursive class κ of formulae there correspond recursive class signs r, such that neither v Gen r nor Neg (v Gen r) belongs to Flg (κ) (where v is the free variable of r)."

Kurt Gödel
On Formally Undecidable Propositions

Gödel was set to be Bound

In Vienna with no one Around

But he couldn't Complete

For the ends would not Meet

As mathematics he found had no Ground

STEPHEN EVANS

Hegel

*"We can only understand by abstracting
and then transcending our abstractions"*

Georg Hegel
The Phenomenology of Spirit

Hegel systemically Taught

Concepts synthetically Thought

Such as abso was Loot

And that history was Moot

So his life was syncretically Fraught

STEPHEN EVANS

Hume

"Generally speaking, the errors in religion are dangerous; those in philosophy only ridiculous."

David Hume
A Treatise of Human Nature

Hume that enquiring Chap

Understood that he needed a Nap

So he took a wee Sip

With empirical Zip

As a Scotsman must have his Nightcap

STEPHEN EVANS

Husserl

"Philosophy—wisdom—is the
philosophizer's quite personal affair"

Edmund Husserl
Cartesian Meditations

Phenomenologically Led

Husserl stayed inside of his Head

But there wasn't much Room

So he took up his Broom

And swept noumena under the Bed

STEPHEN EVANS

Langer

"Art is the objectification of feeling, and the subjectification of nature."

Suzanne Langer
Mind

Suzanne was feeling just Fine
As she signaled the waiter for Wine
While she listened to Bach
And some classical Rock
To hear cymbal and symbol Align

STEPHEN EVANS

Leibniz

*"There is nothing in the understanding
which has not come from the senses, except
the understanding itself, or the one who
understands."*

—Gottfried Leibniz
Philosophical Essays

Leibniz exuded a Moan

When finding himself all Alone

His sighs were the Key

To a Philosophy

That left every moan on its Own

Kant

"I understand by the transcendental idealism of all appearances the doctrine that they are all together to be regarded as mere representations and not things in themselves."

Immanuel Kant
— *Critique of Pure Reason*

Immanuel proffered his Liege
Whose thoughts were noblessly Oblige
That his Mind was Profound
Should his Senses Rebound
Inside Categories under Siege

STEPHEN EVANS

Locke

"I think I may say that of all the men we meet with, nine parts of ten are what they are, good or evil, useful or not, by their education."

John Locke
Thoughts on Education

Locke you should know held the Key
To thinking Empirically
For Knowing he Thought
If his fellows were Taught
They might Finally find themselves Free

STEPHEN EVANS

James

*"First, you know, a new theory is attacked
as absurd; then it is admitted to be true,
but obvious and insignificant; finally it is
seen to be so important that its adversaries
claim that they themselves discovered it."*

—William James
Pragmatism

William was whiling Away
When a squirrel enlivened his Day
As they circled the Tree
Both the rodent and He
Stayed pragmatically dizzy at Bay

Kierkegaard

"The greatest hazard of all, losing one's self, can occur very quietly in the world, as if it were nothing at all."

—Søren Kierkegaard
The Sickness Unto Death

Søren wrote under a Name

That wasn't his own, so his Fame

Would surely Proceed

A bit slowly Indeed

But he made it to Fame just the Same

STEPHEN EVANS

Mill

*"Whatever crushes individuality is despotism,
by whatever name it may be called."*

—John Stuart Mill
On Liberty

Though J Mill was principally Kind
To those who were lesser in Mind
Which included well You
And likely me Too
Toward mankind he simply was Blind

STEPHEN EVANS

Nietzsche

"I entreat you, my brothers, remain true to the earth."

Friedrich Nietzsche
Thus Spoke Zarathustra

The spelling of Nietzsche is Hard

For even a talented Bard

The S and the Z

Are both prior to C

Which the E and the I Disregard

STEPHEN EVANS

Parmenides

"On this road there are very many signs
that being is uncreated and imperishable,
whole, unique, unwavering, and complete."

Parmenides
As quoted by Simplicius

Parmenides hung out with Ze

No his good friend in Ele

A where he Wrote

The first proem of Note

Which I never thought ever could Be

STEPHEN EVANS

Pierce

*"A certain percentage of the human race
are insane and subject to illusions"*

—Charles Sanders Peirce
Selected Philosophical Writings

Pierce was improbably Sure

That his thinking was logically Pure

When not on the Run

He was said to have Fun

With the cenopythagorean Cure

STEPHEN EVANS

Plato

*"They see only their own shadows, or the
shadows of one another, which the fire
throws on the opposite wall of the cave."*

Plato
The Republic

One day Plato got lost in a Cave

And Ideally tried to be Brave

But it altered up his Brain

Likely from the Methane

So he vaulted the cave's Architrave

Pythagoras

"Above all things respect yourself."

— Pythagoras
The Golden Verses

Pythagoras chatting with Buddha
When they met in Nirvana said Who'da
Thought We would Wanna
Ascend to Nirvana
On a musical lotus pad Houdah

Rand

*"To say 'I love you' one must know first
how to say the 'I'."*

—Ayn Rand
The Fountainhead

Ayn Rand it cannot be Said

When writing her own Fountainhead

Was Objectively Clear

To those of us Here

Who dole on the whole Gingerbread

Rousseau

"Man is born free; and everywhere he is in chains."

Jean Rousseau
The Social Contract

Rousseau never thought his Contract

Would have such a rousing Impact

As he fled from the Seine

Of his crime it was Pleine

He was socially out of Contact

Ryle

"Minds are things, but different sorts of things from bodies;"

—Gilbert Ryle
The Concept of Mind

Ryle was giving a Toast

Saying I ain't afraid of no Ghost

Lurking in the Machine

Though he failed to Glean

His machine was a very rude Host

S<small>TEPHEN</small> E<small>VANS</small>

Russell

*"The point of philosophy is to start with
something so simple as not to seem worth
stating, and to end with something so
paradoxical that no one will believe it."*

—Bertrand Russell
The Philosophy of Logical Atomism

Bertrand begin the Decline

Of Philosophy into a Shrine

To the Small and the Snide

As he couldn't Abide

That his Logic would never Align

S<small>TEPHEN</small> E<small>VANS</small>

Sartre

*"I am because I think that I don't want to
be."*

—Jean-Paul Sartre
Nausea

Jean was appallingly Blind

To anything not on his Mind

His existence was Sure

But he had hoped for More

To be sure there was Nothing to Find

STEPHEN EVANS

Schopenhauer

*"The person who writes for fools is always
sure of a large audience."*

—Arthur Schopenhauer
Religion

Arthur was artfully Asked

How a man could be happy Untasked

He said leave me Alone

In an Ominous Tone

I should never have left home Unmasked

Socrates

"That showed me in an instant that not by wisdom do poets write poetry."

Plato
The Apology

Socrates taught—well now, Wait

We don't really know because Plat

O was the One

Who quoted the Son

Of a sculptor, thus Forming his Fate

STEPHEN EVANS

Spinoza

"Every substance is necessarily infinite."

Baruch Spinoza
The Ethics

So one day I was reading Spinoza
And I thought I was reading Sub-Rosa
Till the scheme was Unhatched
And my copy was Snatched
As they took it right under my...Purview

Thales

"Thales thought all things are full of gods."

Aristotle
De Anima

Thales was said to be First
Of the Sages from best to the Worst
His theory that Water
Was all that we Otter
Be came to him in a Cloudburst

Thoreau

*"I have lived some thirty years on this
planet, and I have yet to hear the first
syllable of valuable or even earnest advice
from my seniors."*

Henry Thoreau
Walden

When young Henry set fire to the Wood

Around Concord he hoped that he Could

Extinguish the Blaze

With a record of Days

In a cabin where Emerson Stood

STEPHEN EVANS

Wittgenstein

"'This fellow isn't insane. We are only doing philosophy."

— Ludwig Wittgenstein
On Certainty

Wittgenstein raged at the Thought
That language was something not Nought
He declared with a Rare
Unintelligible Flare
That what cannot be said can be Taught

Stephen Evans

Zeno

"Something about Achilles and a Tortoise"

Zeno
The Legend of Zeno

Zeno was stuck in Elea

Because there was no way to See A

Path he could Travel

His plans would Unravel

So he opened a Greek Pizzeria

About the Author

Stephen Evans is a playwright and the author of *A Transcendental Journey, Painting Sunsets,* and *Funny Thing Is; A Guide to Understanding Comedy.*

Find him online at:

https://www.istephenevans.com/

https://www.facebook.com/iStephenEvans

https://twitter.com/iStephenEvans

https://www.gr8word.com/StephenEvans

STEPHEN EVANS

Books by Stephen Evans

Fiction:

The Marriage of True Minds

Let Me Count the Ways

The Island of Always

Two Short Novels

Painting Sunsets

The Mind of a Writer and other Fables

Non-Fiction:

A Transcendental Journey

Funny Thing Is: A Guide to Understanding Comedy

The Laughing String: Thoughts on Writing

Layers of Light

Liebestraum

STEPHEN EVANS

S<small>TEPHEN</small> E<small>VANS</small>